IMAGES
of America

HOPKINS

IMAGES
of America

HOPKINS

Ann Drayton Lister and
Virginia Hook McCracken

ARCADIA
PUBLISHING

Copyright © 2009 by Ann Drayton Lister and Virginia Hook McCracken
ISBN 978-1-5316-4328-7

Published by Arcadia Publishing
Charleston SC, Chicago IL, Portsmouth NH, San Francisco CA

Library of Congress Control Number: 2009923817

For all general information contact Arcadia Publishing at:
Telephone 843-853-2070
Fax 843-853-0044
E-mail sales@arcadiapublishing.com
For customer service and orders:
Toll-Free 1-888-313-2665

Visit us on the Internet at www.arcadiapublishing.com

*To the citizens of Hopkins, past and present, who have lived
in this small pastoral town and have called it home.*

CONTENTS

ACKNOWLEDGMENTS

We would like to thank the following people and organizations: Marie Barber Adams; Mary Alice Anderson; Debbie Bloom; Linda Claytor Boyer; Rhonda Brown; Marvin Byars; Larry Cameron; Andy Chandler; Jack and Miriam Claytor; Emily McCracken Derrick; Joseph Carlton Derrick; Ray L. Derrick; Eddie Finley; the Congaree National Park; John Gilbert; Tommy Gunter; Marion Hopkins; Mary Ann Hotinger; Carolyn Leitner Huff; Ann McCracken John; Mary Claytor Johnston; Carolyn Karpinos; Mary Barber Kirkland; Paul Hammond Lister; Corrine and Duane Manning; Vickie and Carol McCracken; T. M. McCracken Jr.; Sam and Betty McGregor; Alicia Hayne Mikell; the National Park Service; Sarah Moore; Richland County Public Library; Wehman Sieling; the South Carolina Department of Archives and History; the *South Carolina Wildlife* magazine; the South Caroliniana Library, University of South Carolina; the South East Rural Community Outreach organization; Carla McCracken Schmitt; Harry Spratlin; the *Columbia Star*; J. D. Stocker; Willie Frank Stocker; Tracy Swartout; the Reverend E. Hopkins Weston; Jesse Wheaton; Carrie Barber White; Betty Arrants Whitehead; the Reverend Sam Wade; and Theresa Yednock. Unless otherwise noted, all images appear courtesy of the authors.

INTRODUCTION

Hopkins is a rural community located on the outskirts of South Carolina's state capital. Like many places in the South, Hopkins began primarily as farms, churches, schools, and families. With the inevitable impending commercial growth trickling in from Columbia, farms are being sold for the purposes of subdividing. The acres once filled with livestock, which prevailed in number, have become increasingly sporadic, but the town's homegrown sense of charm remains.

John Hopkins (1739–1775) was one of the earliest large landholders. Hopkins arrived in South Carolina with money and racehorses, likely having sold many of his possessions prior to his arrival. He and his wife, Sarah Thomas Hopkins, followed her family to the state. They arrived in the fall of 1762 and applied for a land grant. They received a grant of 250 acres in 1764 from the king of England. Hopkins's first tract was named Back Swamp. Although it is impossible to now determine its boundaries, the base of an 8-foot chimney remains, marking the homesite. The house was built on an old Native American trail on which a trading post remained until the 1760s. Also on this land is the family cemetery. Hopkins eventually obtained 16 land grants totaling more than 3,000 acres. John Hopkins died of a fever at the young age of 36. His land was left to his sons, one of whom ensured that the town would bear the Hopkins name. Much of his land is still retained by his descendants. Others he remembered in his will were his two orphan nieces who resided with him, the traveling preachers, and the poor. Land grants from the king of England halted in 1776, when the state assumed the right to distribute land ownership. Lands were granted to Europeans, who endeavored to create farms and grazing fields. Flooding temporarily stalled much of the farming but allowed for nutrient renewal in the soil, making it ripe for agricultural activity.

The town of Hopkins was originally called "Hopkins Turnout." The railroad line from Charleston extended only as far as Hopkins. From here, transportation to Columbia was made by stagecoach. The train was turned around on a turntable in order to return to Charleston, thereby giving the town the name Hopkins Turnout. The railroad line to Columbia was completed in 1842.

The Hopkins Presbyterian Church was built in 1891 for the Methodist church, but the congregation did not endure, and so the building was purchased in 1919 for use by the Presbyterians. This is an amazingly well-preserved structure, with the original wooden pews and vestibule still intact. This vernacular church was placed on the National Register of Historic Places in 1986. St. John's Congaree Episcopal Church was established in 1858. The land was donated by Dr. William Weston, and construction on a church building commenced soon after. During that time, services were held at the Elm Savannah schoolhouse, with Rev. Edward Reed presiding. The first service was on July 31, 1858. St. John's was consecrated on November 27th of the same year. Zion Benevolent Baptist Church became a member of the Gethsemane Association Upper Division in 1871. At that time, the church's membership totaled around 68. By 1873, the church's membership exceeded 120 members. The church's first pastor was Rev. Clem P. Davis.

Following the Civil War, St. John Baptist Church was organized by former members of New Light Beulah and New Zion Benevolent Baptist Churches, who had worshipped with the Lower

Richland planters. These planters were members of Beulah Baptist Church, a church founded in 1802. Rev. Samuel Barber started a campaign to organize St. John Baptist Church in Hopkins near Chappell Creek in the early 1870s.

Jerusalem Baptist Church was founded in 1877, and the original structure was built in 1883. Rev. Josh Williams was the founding pastor. The church was rebuilt in 1945, and it was rededicated on July 16, 1995.

The Hicks Chappell House was built in 1781, five years prior to the establishment of Columbia, and it is the oldest dwelling in Richland County. Hicks Chappell, a 19-year-old Virginia native, moved to South Carolina to join the patriot cause during the American Revolution. He was a private with Capt. Robert Goodwyn's Rangers.

The Harriet Barber House is an historic landmark in Hopkins. Through association with the South Carolina Land Commission, the tract of 42.5 acres was deeded to a freed slave in 1872. The Barbers farmed over 24 of the acres, primarily cultivating cotton, and raised 11 children in the home. The dwelling has remained in the Barber family for more than 130 years and continues to serve as a reminder of opportunity for this family. The Richland County Conservation Commission issued a grant allocated for the exterior renovations, including roofing, siding, repair of the front porch, painting, and some structural work. It is currently being used for local meetings and as a special event venue.

Congaree National Park has experienced a metamorphosis of sorts. Its humble beginnings date back to the 16th century, when Congaree Indians inhabited the floodplains. As European settlers came to the area, a smallpox epidemic ran rampant, and the Congaree tribe was greatly reduced. The king of England issued land grants to new residents there until 1776. In 1839, James Adams defined the boundaries for the Congaree Swamp. By the beginning of the 20th century, the Santee River Cypress Lumber Company had bought much of the land for logging; however, flooding and inaccessibility led to inoperable working conditions, and within 10 years, operations were abandoned. The floodplains were virtually untouched during those years, and the swamp remained a natural habitat. In 1974, a portion of the swamp was renamed the Congaree National Monument and was registered as a Natural Historical Landmark. It was declared an International Biosphere Reserve in June 1983 and a Globally Important Bird Area in 2001. In 2003, it became the 57th national park. This world-class biosphere is becoming increasingly popular as a tourist destination due to its exceptional biodiversity.

Hopkins is rich in history, tradition, and preservation. The many families, homes, and structures speak volumes about Hopkins's past, and the desire of many to chronicle its past has been evident throughout the pursuit of this publication. We aspire for this to be an accurate glimpse into the images of Hopkins.

One

THE HOPKINS COMMUNITY

FAMILIES AND TRADITIONS

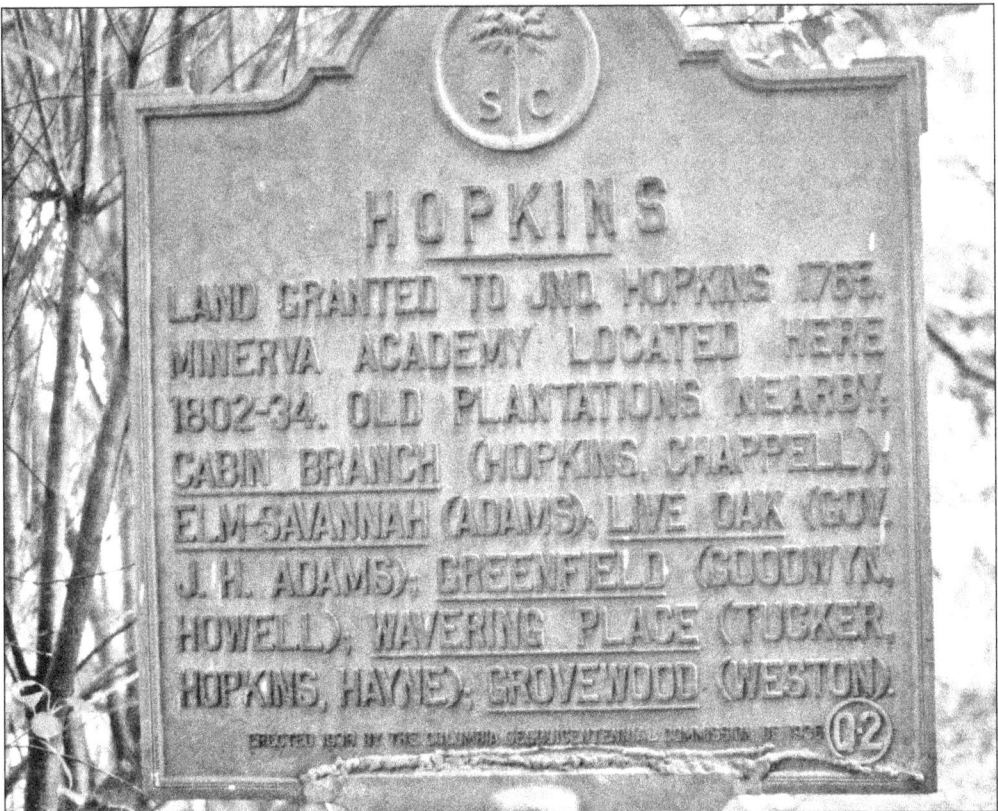

This historical marker, located near the Hopkins Post Office, was erected by the Richland County Sesquicentennial Commission in 1936. It lists many of the families in this book who were early settlers in the community, as well as the names of their homes. Also noted is Minerva Academy, a school considered to have had a reputation for high academic standards.

The depot, shops, and businesses that once made up the small village of Hopkins are no longer there. Trains still pass through several times each day, but these are freight trains, not the passenger trains that were so vital to the community 100 years ago. It is this small community, once a village, that is introduced in this book. Hopkins residents gladly share their old photographs and memories with a sense of nostalgia, reflection, pride, and humor.

Hopkins today is a rural community spread out over many miles. The old town of Hopkins's identity was diminished for many, except those who live and work near the old town. Efforts are under way to research Hopkins's history and share the findings with the community. The South East Rural Community Outreach (SERCO) organization is working to preserve the history of not only Hopkins, but also many of the other small communities that comprise the lower part of Richland County, or, as it is called today, the Lower Richland community.

Initially, a few wealthy planters owned huge land grants and slaves who worked the land. After the Civil War, almost everyone had a family farm used for both income and sustenance. Corn was a versatile crop planted by many farmers to provide food for their families and livestock.

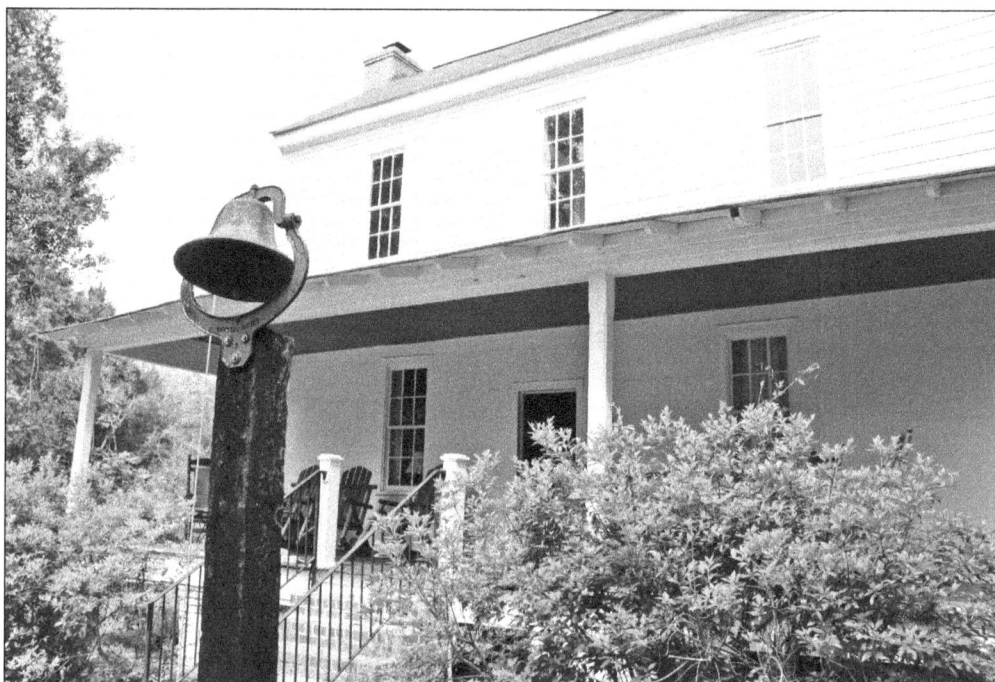

Nineteen-year-old Virginian Hicks Chappell came to South Carolina and joined the fight for American independence. A private with Capt. Robert Goodwyn's Rangers, he later became a major. Chappell built the Hicks Chappell House in 1781, which is pictured above. (Courtesy of the *Columbia Star*.)

Shown at left in this 1945 photograph is Charles T. Smith Jr., the husband of Jessie Chappell, who was the great-granddaughter of Hicks Chappell. It was Charles who rescued the bell shown in the above photograph from a home in Pond Bluff before that area was flooded to form Lake Marion. (Courtesy of the *Columbia Star*.)

This 1940 photograph shows just one of the many old homesites on Pond Bluff just before the area was inundated by Lake Marion. (Courtesy of the *Columbia Star*.)

Chappell was named one of Richland County's first judges and eventually filled Wade Hampton's seat in the House of Representatives when Hampton became sheriff. Upon Chappell's death in 1836, he left the house, land, servants, and all belongings to his wife, Elizabeth Threewits. The income generated by the farm was divided equally between his wife and two sons, John Joel Chappell and James Henry Chappell. (Courtesy of the *Columbia Star*.)

Descendants of the Chappells always occupied the home. Septima "Seppie" Smith and her sister, Claudia (1897–1976), lived in the home until Seppie's death in 1986. Seppie was a longtime schoolteacher at the Schneider School, of which she authored a history. The first floor of the home had a library, a formal dining room, and a parlor; on the second floor there were four bedrooms. Like many houses then, the kitchen and outhouse were on outlying areas. The family later added a front porch and additional rooms. There was also an attic for storage. (Courtesy of the *Columbia Star*.)

On July 23, 2008, lightning struck the Hicks Chappell House, and the wooden structure quickly burned to the ground. The loss of this historic landmark caused grief to the family, but they plan to rebuild on the land where their 227-year-old home once stood. (Both, courtesy of the *Columbia Star*.)

Cabin Branch was built prior to 1800 by the second John Hopkins. There was a large chimney in the house, rooms downstairs, and two small attic rooms. The original kitchen was not attached to the house. The back part of the house, added later, was elevated, while the front was built on solid ground. During the Civil War, Union soldiers tore out the bricks from the back of the house and dug up the basement in search of gold or silver they thought might have been hidden there. The family said that when the wind blew, the back part of the house would shake as a result of the destruction by the Union soldiers. (Courtesy of the Reverend E. Hopkins Weston.)

This picture shows the home of Dr. Jim Hopkins and his wife, Grace Weston Hopkins. They had one son named Thomas, who married Katherine "Kate" Palmer from Charleston, South Carolina. Kate and Tom built their own home on the family property where they raised their eight children. (Courtesy of Marion Hopkins.)

The original home of Dr. Jim and Grace Hopkins was remodeled and expanded, and in later years became the home of Dr. Tiff and Mary Claytor, who eventually moved to Barnwell, South Carolina. (Courtesy of Marion Hopkins.)

This is a picture of Dr. Jim Hopkins's house as it looks today, having been remodeled once more. The house was rented for a number of years prior to being sold to Dr. Tiff Claytor. It no longer belongs to the Hopkins family.

Oldfield, a plantation belonging to the Hopkins family, was part of a land grant made to John Hopkins in 1775. This was once the summer home of John Hopkins and his family. Oldfield was inherited by James Hopkins (1773–1844) and was later willed to his daughter, Keziah Goodwyn Hopkins Brevard. (Courtesy of the Reverend E. Hopkins Weston.)

Oldfield was rebuilt in the late 1790s by James Hopkins, the son of John Hopkins and father to Keziah Goodwyn Brevard Hopkins. It was made up of three rooms and an adjacent kitchen. Oldfield was then about 50 feet west of the present house. This home was later destroyed by fire. (Courtesy of the Reverend E. Hopkins Weston.)

The third Oldfield home was built in 1805. The sandstone steps are all that remain to mark the entrance of the house that was burned in 1865 by Gen. William T. Sherman's troops. This was probably the birthplace of Gov. James Hopkins Adams (1812–1861), who spent much of his childhood there. (Courtesy of the Reverend E. Hopkins Weston.)

Oldfield was rebuilt by English Hopkins immediately after a 1902 fire. Some of the furniture was salvaged by throwing it through the windows and later carrying it to safety. The document showing the original grant from the king of England to John Hopkins was lost, however. English Hopkins is pictured here in front of Oldfield with his wife, Laura Jervey Smith Hopkins. This photograph was taken in the late 1800s. (Courtesy of the Reverend E. Hopkins Weston.)

This picture, taken around 1900, shows English Hopkins (far right, man with beard) and others standing in one of his cotton fields at Oldfield. Oldfield was again destroyed, this time by the Horrell Hill tornado of April 30, 1924. The tornado left a 135-mile path of devastation, the longest in the state's history. It began in Aiken County and ended in Darlington County. The death toll was 67 people, with over half living in Richland County and most of those living in Horrell Hill, a neighboring town to Hopkins. Giant oak trees were uprooted and laid fallen on the ground. Buildings were carried off the ground, swept away, and left in broken heaps. This tornado would be classified by today's standards as an F4, with wind speeds ranging from 207 to 260 miles per hour. (Courtesy of the Reverend E. Hopkins Weston.)

The original Oldfield plantation was a log cabin built by John Hopkins in 1770. This place was used as a summer home. The cabin faced north and was positioned about 100 feet north of the present house. This is a picture of Oldfield from the 1950s. (Courtesy of the Reverend E. Hopkins Weston.)

The Oldfield that stands today was built immediately following the 1924 tornado. It was occupied by the family on Thanksgiving Day, 1924. Members of the Hopkins family maintain the house and grounds, often entertaining there. Large oak trees line both sides of the long driveway into Oldfield, creating a lovely and graceful entrance to the fifth house built on this property, which has belonged to the Hopkins family since 1775. (Courtesy of the Reverend E. Hopkins Weston.)

Keziah Goodwin Hopkins Brevard was the largest female landowner in the area. Three of her residences were burned during Gen. William T. Sherman's march. These included a house in town, located on the corner of Bull and Blanding Streets in Columbia, a gristmill at Adams Pond in Hopkins, and her birthplace, Oldfield plantation. Kizzie, as she was known to her family, spent much of her time at Alwehav, her home in the Sandhills. This is where she lived during the time that her other residences were under siege. She wrote a diary of the Civil War in 1863 that was recently edited and published. She died in 1886 at the age of 83 years. This photograph is of Adams Pond, where Keziah Goodwin Hopkins Brevard's gristmill once stood.

The house pictured here was built in 1918 by Christian Tucker Weston just prior to his marriage. Pine trees from the land were cut and split to make this home. He added a front porch and a sleeping porch to the house after rebuilding from damage done by the tornado in April 1924. (Courtesy of the Reverend E. Hopkins Weston.)

Rosa Lee Davis, pictured here, was affectionately known as "Peach." She worked as a cook for the Weston family for many years. This photograph was taken at the Weston home on Elm Savannah Road. (Courtesy of the Reverend E. Hopkins Weston.)

This is an early picture of the house Christian Tucker Weston built in 1918 prior to his marriage to Mary Postell Hopkins. It is still occupied by a member of the Hopkins family. (Courtesy of the Reverend E. Hopkins Weston.)

In 1872, Samuel Barber purchased lot no. 35, containing 42.5 acres of land, from the South Carolina Land Commission for redistribution. This was a rare opportunity for a former slave turned freedman to become a landowner. His wife, Harriet, was also once a slave. Harriet made the final payment in 1879, receiving the title to the property, and the house now bears her name. (Courtesy of the South Carolina Department of Archives and History.)

The land and Harriet Barber House have remained in the same family since 1872. After the death of Samuel (1891) and Harriet (1899), their son John and daughter-in-law Mamie Holley took up residence there. They raised 11 children in this historic home. Its significance qualified it for one of the first awards disbursed by Richland County's grant program for preservation. (Courtesy of the South Carolina Department of Archives and History.)

On May 1, 2006, the Richland County Conservation Commission issued a grant to the Harriet Barber House in the amount of $25,000. The grant provided funds for roofing, siding, front porch repair, painting, and various other structural works. An additional grant of $37,500 was issued on May 25, 2007, to complete the exterior changes. The family is now using the house to better the community. Celebrations, meetings, and lectures are held there regularly. Some of these events include a Heritage Day celebration, a Memorial Day celebration, and a Christmas tour. Local dignitaries, artisans, and musicians are often featured. The home has been featured in numerous articles and interviews for the family's preservation efforts.

John Barber began teaching at Hopkins Elementary School in 1919. This was the same school he had gone to as a boy, although the location had changed. He retired in 1941. In this same year his son, Ulysses, became a teacher, principal, and coach at the very same school. This picture shows a side view of the Harriet Barber House, where John Barber lived and raised his family. (Courtesy of the South Carolina Department of Archives and History.)

Naomi Daniels Jackson is holding WeTonia Barber in front of the Harriet Barber House. WeTonia was the granddaughter of Rev. John B. and Mamie Barber. The boy is unidentified. This photograph of the Harriet Barber House was taken in the late 1940s. (Courtesy of the Barber family photograph collection.)

The Harriet Barber House is a one-story structure built with weatherboard siding. Many additions were made to the home, doubling the size of the building. The family has enjoyed increasing prosperity throughout the past century, building on the hard work and opportunity of their ancestors. This landmark was added to the National Register of Historic Places on March 27, 1986. (Courtesy of the South Carolina Department of Archives and History.)

This picture shows one of the remaining outer buildings on the property of the historic Harriet Barber House. (Courtesy of the South Carolina Department of Archives and History.)

Mary Barber Kirkland (left) and her twin sister, Carrie Barber White, are the children pictured here riding a tricycle. They are the children of Ulysses and Ann Barber, granddaughters of John and Mamie Barber, and great-granddaughters of Samuel and Harriett Barber. These young ladies were born and raised in Hopkins, along with their sisters Jean and Marie. In more recent years, the Barber sisters have worked tirelessly to preserve the Harriet Barber House and its history. (Courtesy of the Barber family photograph collection.)

Alice Barber is pictured here. She was the wife of Henry, John Barber's half-brother. (Courtesy of the Barber family photograph collection.)

Russell Hagood married Mable Barber Hagood, who was the daughter of Rev. John and Mamie Barber. He was a carpenter, businessman, and driver. He traveled to Pittsburg, Pennsylvania, in the summers and sold watermelons that were grown in South Carolina there. (Courtesy of the Barber family photograph collection.)

This photograph of James Middleton (right) and his friends was taken in front of an early touring car. Touring cars were popular in the early 20th century. These cars, larger alternatives to the roadster and runabout models, were typically open and featured a convertible top. Side curtains could be installed to protect passengers from the elements. (Courtesy of the Barber family photograph collection.)

Mamie Holley Barber and Rev. John B. Barber lived on Lower Richland Boulevard, a short distance from the old Hopkins Turnout depot. They had 11 children. Mamie, pictured above reading, had a twin sister, Lillie. Their mother was Charlotte Sumter, formerly of Chappell plantation. Mamie was said to be the more reserved twin. (Courtesy of the Barber family photograph collection.)

Many old photographs were found by the family in the historic Harriet Barber House. The couple in this photograph is unidentified. (Courtesy of the Barber family photograph collection.)

Lillie (left) and Mamie Holley were the twin daughters of Charlotte Sumter and Richard Holley. Mamie married Rev. John B. Barber and lived all of her life in Hopkins, and Lillie married Sam McCoy of Hopkins. Following Sam's death, Lillie remarried and lived in Prosperity, South Carolina. After they were married, the twins took turns visiting each other every other year on their birthday, July 1st. (Courtesy of the Barber family photograph collection.)

This photograph, taken around 1920, shows four young men standing in front of two sporty cars. Were they going to church or to a Friday night dance? Perhaps they would drive to Columbia to see a movie. Wherever these four dapper men were headed, they were dressed for the occasion. Pictured from left to right are unidentified, Jesse Bush, Thomas McCracken Sr., and unidentified. (Courtesy of T. M. McCracken Jr.)

Dr. Hubert Claytor came to South Carolina from Maryland in 1883 on a request for physicians to help during an epidemic. Dr. Claytor lived in this house for 60 years and practiced medicine here. This photograph was taken in 1965, when the house was unoccupied. (Courtesy of Linda Claytor Boyer.)

Virginia Claytor Manning and her husband, Gerry, began renovating and restoring the Claytor house in 1976, completing most of the work themselves. Virginia, who was the granddaughter of Dr. Hubert Claytor, grew up in the house and lived there until her marriage. Renovations included converting Dr. Claytor's office into a sunporch and making the original smokehouse into a small guesthouse. The interior and exterior are constructed of heart pine. The Queen Anne home was placed on the Richland County Bicentennial Committee's register of historic homes. (Courtesy of Jack Claytor and Miriam Claytor.)

This photograph shows the Murphy-McCracken home, which was built in 1881. John Henry and Emma McCracken raised 10 children here. It was originally constructed with two connected rooms and an adjacent kitchen. Over the years, it was added onto, and it remains in the McCracken family. The land is still farmed for personal use.

This picture shows a snowfall in Hopkins, which is rare. Winters are mild, with occasional low temperatures in the teens. Along with the cold rains in the winter, an occasional ice storm causes tree limbs to break and power lines to fall. The majority of residents in the Hopkins area get their water from wells with electric pumps. When they lose electric power, they also lose water. This situation can also occur in summer months when thunderstorms with high winds down power lines.

Always an animal lover, Carlton McCracken, a son of John Henry and Emma McCracken, is shown in a "swept yard" in 1925 with his favorite hunting dog, Speed. The youngest of the 10 McCracken children, he lived his entire life in Hopkins, having been born and raised in the Murphy-McCracken house. He operated a dairy, raised beef cattle, and farmed.

Carolyn Leitner Huff (right) chases butterflies with a cousin outside of the Murphy-McCracken home in the 1950s. This was the home of their grandparents, John Henry McCracken and Emma Murphy McCracken. It was customary for children and grandchildren to return home after church on Sunday afternoons. (Courtesy of Carolyn Leitner Huff.)

This photograph of Meeting House plantation was taken in 1898. The original house was built by Joel Adams (1750–1830). Pictured from left to right are Grace Weston Adams Davis, Annie Eliza Gorman Clarkson, James Adams Clarkson Jr., Peter Castor, James Adams Clarkson Sr., Dr. Hubert Claytor, Edward McCrady Claytor, and Johnson Adams. (Courtesy of Mary Ann Hotinger.)

The Meeting House was originally two separate buildings used to hold church services and instruction for slaves in the area. Grace Weston Adams Davis had the two buildings connected and was the first person to live in the house. Davis was married, but her brothers did not approve of her husband and strongly suggested to him that he should leave the county. (Courtesy of Mary Ann Hotinger.)

The Meeting House was renovated in 1987 by a descendant of Annie Eliza Gorman Clarkson. The house was modernized in the renovation but has maintained its history and its original charm. The grounds have been landscaped in keeping with the history of the home, and it is surrounded by beautiful trees from which hangs Spanish moss. (Courtesy of Mary Ann Hotinger.)

Grace Weston Adams Davis did not have any surviving children; her only child died in infancy. She took on one of her brother's children to raise as her own. This child was Annie Eliza Gorman. The name was formerly O'Gorman but was shortened to Gorman upon her family's arrival in the United States. (Courtesy of Mary Ann Hotinger.)

This greenhouse, also shown in the back left of the 1898 photograph of the Meeting House on page 38, was a wedding present to Annie Eliza Gorman. It has been restored by the family and is used today by the present occupants, who are descendants of Gorman. (Courtesy of Mary Ann Hotinger.)

In the early 1900s, George W. Arrants came to Hopkins, where he met Alberta Spigner, whose father was the stationmaster. They were married in 1906, and for about the next 50 years, they lived here, raising a family of two daughters and five sons who were active in the community life of Hopkins. (Courtesy of Betty Arrants Whitehead.)

This is a picture of the Arrants house from the 1940s. The present residents are diligent in keeping the house well maintained. Beside the home is a lovely flower garden and fountain. In the spring, beautiful azaleas bloom in profusion, and throughout the year, seasonal flowers add color to this spot. (Courtesy of Betty Arrants Whitehead.)

Wehman Sieling is shown playing in front of the barn at the home of his grandparents, Jeremiah Glenn and Annie Lee McCracken Cook. Wehman is the son of Jerry and Dorothy Cook Sieling. Annie Lee, the oldest of 10 children, bred and sold registered chihuahuas, and at one time her husband ran a shingle mill in Hopkins. Jeremiah Cook was also a farmer, raised cattle, and was a logger. He cut logs in Cook's Swamp, which he owned. The logs were hauled to the Wateree River, where they were lashed together in a cartwheel shape. Cook rode the logs down the rivers to the mill in Charleston and caught the train, the *Carolina Special*, back to Hopkins. (Courtesy of Wehman Sieling.)

Children spent much of their recreational time outdoors. Shown here catching a football is Jesse Wheaton as a young boy, playing in the backyard at the home of Annie Lee and Jeremiah Cook. Jesse Wheaton lived nearby in the Hicks Chappell House. (Courtesy of Wehman Sieling.)

Two

Religion and Education
Historical Hopkins Schools
and Churches

Established in 1858, St. John's Episcopal Church was built on land donated by Dr. William Weston. During the time of its construction, services were held at the Elm Savannah schoolhouse. The first service was on July 31, 1858. St. John's was consecrated on November 27th of the same year. St. John's Episcopal Church was established to serve families who lived within a buggy-ride's distance.

This photograph was taken following a 1943 wedding at St. John's Episcopal Church. A rectory was built in 1957 and a parish house in 1965. The parish house was expanded again in 1996 and in 2001. (Courtesy of Mary Claytor Johnston.)

Plans for improvements were under way at the end of 1981. An architect and member of the vestry took measurements just before Christmas, and plans were in place to apply for funding from the Columbia Historical Society. St. John's burned to the ground on December 26, 1981, due to a furnace malfunction; arson was never suspected. The heart-pine construction provided immediate kindling.

The church was rebuilt using the original plans, an almost exact reproduction of the previous building. The new church is 20 percent larger and made of white pine and cypress. The handsome stained-glass windows were replicated by the same firm that made the originals. Approximately 125 families are currently members of St. John's, with an average attendance of 110 at two services each Sunday.

Gov. James Hopkins Adams was baptized at St. John's Episcopal Church. He lived at Live Oak plantation, which is now inside the McEntire Air National Guard Base. He was elected a state senator in 1850 and South Carolina governor in 1854. His tombstone still towers in the St. John's cemetery.

The Presbyterian congregation, formed in the late 1800s, originally met in a nearby school building. Following the transfer of land from the Methodists in 1918, the Presbyterians acquired an additional 1.5 acres. Dr. J. R. Hopkins and Angus McGregor, trustees representing the Presbyterian church, signed the deed. (Courtesy of the South Carolina Department of Archives and History.)

The building that is now the Hopkins Presbyterian Church was originally built in 1891 for the members of Hopkins Methodist Church. The land was acquired from Nancy L. Bush. After worshipping there for about 25 years, the Methodists sold the building to a group of Hopkins Presbyterians in 1918.

A Columbia Presbyterian Seminary student led services twice a month until the church was formally organized in 1916. The intimate group of 15 charter members grew to a congregation of 41 by 1937. A. P. Toomer was the first pastor of Hopkins Presbyterian Church. Several other fine ministers, including Dr. Hugh R. Murchison and Dr. F. Ray Riddle, served at this church.

In 1965, the Congaree Presbytery deeded the property to the Hopkins Presbyterian Church Cemetery Association, which was formed to maintain the church and grounds. On the markers in the church cemetery are found the names of relatives of the Bush, McCracken, Mustard, Gorman, Fraylick, and Williamson families. Hopkins Presbyterian Church remains a remarkably intact example of a small rural church from the 19th century. This original structure remains well maintained and echoes a tribute to yesteryear. (Courtesy of the South Carolina Department of Archives and History.)

Among the graves in the Hopkins Presbyterian Cemetery are three, for a mother and two children, who were killed in the April 30, 1924, tornado. This storm left a 130-mile path of destruction from Aiken to Richland County and would, by today's standards, have been classified as an F4. Winds averaged from 207 to 260 miles per hour. Many families have been laid to rest here, including some of the church's charter members.

A number of generations have worshipped at Jerusalem Baptist Church. This church was founded in 1877. In 1883, the first sanctuary was constructed. The founding pastor was Rev. Josh Williams. A plaque on the side of the church states that it was rebuilt in 1945 and rededicated on July 16, 1995. Today the pastor is Rev. Patrick A. Harrin.

On the edge of the Congaree National Park stands Mt. Moriah Baptist Church. The church pictured above is a building that was an early sanctuary. Behind this building is the church cemetery. This cemetery is surrounded by large beautiful live oak trees that are heavily draped with Spanish moss. Across the road from this building is the large sanctuary that serves the congregation today.

The Myers Cemetery was virtually forgotten until Bluff Road was straightened. Old Bluff Road forks to the right off Bluff Road and is nearer to the Congaree River than Bluff Road. The Myers Cemetery can now be seen from Bluff Road during the winter. Visibility and access to the walled cemetery is difficult in warmer months due to overgrown vegetation.

There are several graves marked with headstones in the Myers Cemetery, along with what appears to be sites of unmarked graves. Of these unmarked graves, one is believed to be the grave of a young girl, around 14 years old, who died of typhoid fever in the mid-1800s and another the grave of a 10-year-old boy who drowned about the same time.

One marked grave of particular interest is that of Col. David Myers. His tombstone states that he "was born near this place on the 29th November 1768 and was inhumanly murdered by John McLemore on the 3rd of March 1835." He was also said to be one of the first planters in the area.

Different versions of the death of Col. David Myers exist. One story is that he was the victim of a duel. Others claim that he was killed over a boundary dispute. While digging a ditch, a man told Myers that if he was still digging the ditch when the man returned from Columbia, the man was going to kill him. When the man returned, Colonel Myers was indeed still digging the ditch and was shot by the same man. No one knows for certain except that he was "inhumanly murdered by John McLemore on the 3rd of March 1835."

Goodwyn's Cemetery is the burial place of members of the Goodwyn family, their slaves, and the descendants of their slaves. There is no easy access to this cemetery. It is on private property, is hard to find, requires permission to enter the locked gate, and requires a long walk on uneven ground.

Shown here is another picture of Goodwyn's Cemetery. There are many graves here. Numerous graves are marked with headstones. Some of these headstones are ornately carved, while others are marked more simply. There is evidence of many unmarked graves. Interest has been shown in doing research on this cemetery and its history, as well as trying to determine who may be buried here.

This photograph depicts the site of a government burial ground for African American soldiers, veterans, and their immediate families. It is located behind St. John Baptist Church. Sometime after 1945, a farmer dismantled the cemetery. He tossed the headstones into a nearby creek, and the land was used for farming. In 1997, the 2.09 acres was donated by the C. W. Haynes and Company to St. John Baptist Church. Volunteers have been able to recover 28 of the headstones, which are now properly preserved on the site. St. John Baptist Church diligently and respectfully maintains this important historical site with hopes of retrieving the remaining markers from the creek.

St. John Baptist Church was organized immediately after the Civil War by members who had previously worshipped with the Lower Richland planters. The Reverend Samuel Barber initiated an effort to organize St. John Baptist Church in Hopkins. Ephraim Neal gave land for the first church building. The first preacher called to serve the church was Rev. Phillip Shiver, and Rev. William Lowman became the first ordained minister on December 1, 1875. Rev. Jesse W. Neal became pastor in 1893 and served for 51 years. Rev. Westberry H. Neal, Rev. Jesse Neal's son, succeeded his father and served for 58 years. The church is still active today and is pastored by Rev. Sammy L. Wade.

The Community House was a building used by residents of the Hopkins area for various meetings, both business and social. It became popular as a place where the young people of the community often gathered on Friday nights to dance to the music of a good band made up of a trio of adults who lived in Hopkins. (Courtesy of the South Carolina Department of Archives and History.)

Hopkins Graded School, built around 1897, was a one-room schoolhouse serving the local white families. A growing number of attendees prompted the construction of a two-story school across the road in 1914. The graded school is a uniquely undamaged example of a small, rural school from the late 19th century. (Courtesy of the South Carolina Department of Archives and History.)

This one-story building has an L-shaped frame with weatherboard siding and a gable roof. On the roof ridge is a small, square belfry with a pyramid-shaped roof. Two brick chimneys crest the ridge on the north side. The roofing is made from modern sheet metal. It was listed on the National Register of Historic Places on March 27, 1986. (Courtesy of the South Carolina Department of Archives and History.)

The Hopkins Graded School, also known as the Old Hopkins School, is historically significant for its role in education in Hopkins at the beginning of the 20th century. Following the move to the two-story building, the original Hopkins Graded School was used as a teacherage. Its first occupants were the principal and his family. (Courtesy of the South Carolina Department of Archives and History.)

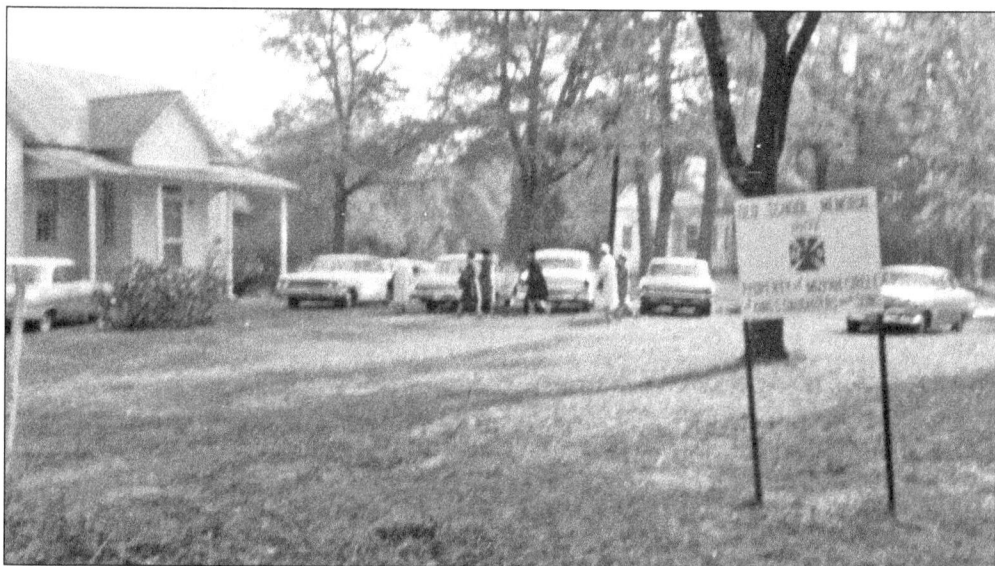

In the late 1800s, this building was a two-room schoolhouse. When a new school was built nearby, this one was known as "the Teacherage" because two of the teachers resided here. In 1916, a group of Hopkins women organized the Mizpah Circle of the International Order of the King's Daughters and Sons, a philanthropic organization. When the Teacherage was no longer needed by the school system, Mizpah Circle acquired it, and it was called the Old School Memorial for a time. After 92 years, the Mizpah Circle is still an active group striving to promote the welfare of the Hopkins community. Here women are gathering for one of their meetings at the Old School Memorial. The King's Daughters and Sons sign is visible in the yard. (Courtesy of the South Carolina Department of Archives and History.)

This 1935 photograph of the Hopkins School is from a collection of fire insurance pictures housed at the South Carolina Department of Archives and History. This two-story building was constructed in 1914 across the road from the old Hopkins Graded School. The old school building was no longer large enough for the number of students attending. The first floor of the building was entered through a central front door from a front porch. There was one classroom to the left of a central hall and an identical classroom across the hall on the right. The central hall went to the back of the school, where an auditorium was located. Down the hall to the left of the auditorium was a girls' restroom, and to the right of the auditorium was a stairway to the second floor. Under the stage was a bin where coal was kept to use in the potbellied stoves in each classroom. The second floor was identical to the ground floor, with two classrooms on either side of a hallway and a boys' restroom directly above the girls' restroom. (Courtesy of the South Carolina Department of Archives and History.)

This 1922 photograph of the Hopkins School shows the student body standing in front of the building in the garden C. B. Epting, the principal, always planted. Many students who attended the school remember with particular fondness the sweet peas from the garden, which can be seen in this picture. The time of year must have been late spring—almost time for school to let out for the summer—since the sweet peas are blooming and the children are barefoot. One student remembers a recess activity the young boys engaged in: there was a small ledge on the building about 2 feet above the ground that went around the entire building. The boys would try to stay on the ledge and inch their way around the building without falling off.

This photograph shows the gymnasium of Lower Richland High School, which was built in 1941 by the Works Progress Administration, started by Franklin Delano Roosevelt. Lower Richland High School is on Lower Richland Boulevard and is home to an International Baccalaureate program. Lower Richland is also the recipient of a Smaller Learning Communities Literacy Grant. (Courtesy of the South Carolina Department of Archives and History.)

In 1924, many of the community schools in the area agreed to merge to establish Consolidated High School No. 1. In 1940, a new name for the school was sought, and ideas were submitted for consideration. "Lower Richland High School," submitted by Edward Mustard, a student, was selected. (Courtesy of the South Carolina Department of Archives and History.)

This is the Hopkins School, where Rev. John B. Barber became the teaching principal in 1923. Rooms were later added to the back of the building. Reverend Barber's son, Ulysses Barber, became the teaching principal in 1941. The school building is still located on Clarkson Road but has been converted into a church. This is from the 1935 Fire Insurance Photo Collection from the South Carolina Department of Archives and History.

Ulysses Barber, affectionately known as Professor Barber, was the son of Rev. John B. Barber and Mamie Holley Barber. His grandparents were Rev. Samuel Barber and Harriet Barber. After graduating from Allen University, he became a teacher at the Waverley School in Columbia. The next year, he became the teaching principal at the Hopkins School. (Courtesy of the Barber family photograph collection.)

In 1955, Ulysses Barber became the first principal of a fully accredited black school. Although he enjoyed his position as principal, his passion was for teaching. Barber returned to teaching at the Gadsden Elementary School and remained there until retirement. He was awarded Teacher of the Year at Gadsden Elementary in 1972 and was named Teacher of the Year for Richland District One the following year. The Hopkins Middle School named its new gymnasium in his honor. Ulysses Barber was the recipient of numerous awards throughout his profession and was a well-respected member of the Hopkins community. He is pictured at far right in this 1945 photograph. (Courtesy of the Barber family photograph collection.)

Recently, a new auditorium was built at the Hopkins Middle School, formerly the Hopkins High School. This new building is named the Ulysses R. Barber Auditorium, and his picture is prominently displayed inside. The Hopkins High School was built in 1954, and Barber was the first principal. After being open for just a few years, there were more than 1,000 students in attendance.

Three

INDUSTRY
BACKBONE OF THE
HOPKINS COMMUNITY

The town of Hopkins was originally called "Hopkins Turnout." The railroad line from Charleston extended only as far as Hopkins, where the trains were turned around on a turntable for the trip back to Charleston. From Hopkins Turnout, transportation to Columbia was by stagecoach. The railroad line to Columbia was complete in 1842. (Courtesy of Wehman Sieling.)

The Hopkins Turnout Depot was constructed in 1834. It was located near the intersection of Back Swamp Road and Lower Richland Boulevard. This station was built following the abandonment of the Minervaville site in 1834. This was also the location of the first Hopkins Post Office. Stationmaster W. Q. Collins is pictured in this 1931 photograph. (Courtesy of John Gilbert.)

Cotton was sold by farmers on platforms at the Hopkins Turnout Depot. The cotton was examined for quality and weighed, and a price was determined. When the depot burned, many farmers had to transport their crops to the neighboring town of Eastover. Travel could be difficult and expensive, even to a nearby town, but for a period of time was necessary. (Courtesy of Wehman Sieling.)

Trains that came through Hopkins did not stop to pick up the mail. Instead, the mailbag was hung from a metal pole. When the train came by, a lever would drop a metal arm to retrieve the mailbag and reel it into the train. Occasionally, the metal arm would miss, and the mailbag would be dragged beneath the train as far as Charleston. (Courtesy of Wehman Sieling.)

The railroad track has always been a place for people to gather to wait for a ride to see friends and to sell their produce. People often sold their produce from the back of their trucks. This picture from the early 1950s shows a man relaxing for a moment where the depot once stood. (Courtesy of Wehman Sieling.)

Shipping cotton to markets in Charleston became much less difficult and less expensive with the railroad system. The terminal point at Hopkins Turnout was a convenient way to transport harvests. Cotton production was distressed in 1917 due to the ruinous effects of the boll weevil. By 1922, cotton revenue was down more than 70 percent.

Robert Mustard stands beside Mustard's General Store. In the picture can be seen the front porch of the store and the square facade above the roof of the porch. The sign on the side of the store indicates there is a telephone inside. A railroad house can be seen in the background. This was the home of the section foreman for the Southern Railroad and was owned by the railroad. (Courtesy of T. M. McCracken Jr.)

William Bryant and Olie Mustard came from Charleston to Hopkins with two children. They ran a grocery and hardware store called Mustard's General Store. They had five more children, and all were raised behind the store, where they made their home. One of their grandsons, Thomas Murphy McCracken Jr., is pictured beside the store in Olie Mustard's flower garden. (Courtesy of T. M. McCracken Jr.)

Raymond Mustard, the son of Olie and William Mustard, is shown standing behind Mustard's General Store in this 1925 photograph. The steps lead to the Mustards' home at the back of the store. Gorman's General Store is shown in the background. Mustard's and Gorman's both sold general merchandise, meat, canned goods, farm supplies (such as plow points), and seed. Gorman's also sold fertilizer by the ton. (Courtesy of T. M. McCracken Jr.)

Little Tamplet Mustard is shown playing behind the Mustard and Gorman stores in 1925. The buildings in this picture are smaller structures on the property of the Gorman residence. The photographer would have had his back to the stores and railroad track, and Tamplet would be facing the tracks. (Courtesy of T. M. McCracken Jr.)

Olie Mustard is all smiles in this picture as she is hugged by her son, John Pearce Mustard. Bootsie, as he was called, had just returned home after serving four years in the army during World War II. During his time in the army, Bootsie fought in the Battle of the Bulge. William and Olie Mustard had four sons who fought in World War II, and all four returned home safely. (Courtesy of T. M. McCracken Jr.)

Dried beans and peas were kept in drawers and sold. Meat trucks would deliver large sides of beef, and the Mustards would carve the meat. They also sold large sacks of flour and meal. Grocery distributors would come to the store for orders and would deliver the groceries in two to three days. William Bryant Mustard (1873–1953) and Olie Georgia Pearce Mustard (1886–1949) are pictured behind their store. (Courtesy of T. M. McCracken Jr.)

This photograph shows Hopkins as it looked in 1950. Mustard's General Store is no longer there.
The store in the center of the picture was built by Olie and William Mustard's youngest son,
Edward, and was operated by their grandson, Carol McCracken. The car out front is Carol's 1948
Mercury convertible. Next to this building is one belonging to Titus Kye, and next to it is a small
sandwich shop owned and operated by Phyllis Alston. Behind Alston's shop was a leather shop

owned and operated by Joe Sumter, although it is not visible in the photograph. There was also a livery stable where a blacksmith shoed horses and mules. In the background stands a tall, white house that was home to some of the John Gorman family. The large building on the far left is Gorman's store, which was no longer in operation. (Courtesy of Wehman Sieling.)

In the early days, small farms were prevalent. Hopkins boasted fertile land for growing many crops, and this proved to be advantageous for the region. Over the years, as new equipment and methods emerged, many of the small farms gave way to larger ones.

The natural environment of Hopkins is conducive to farming. Warm summers and mild winters, coupled with rich soil (from which the county, Richland, acquired its name) make for ideal planting conditions. Farms were prevalent in the area, with many people coming from the coast to increase their earnings as farmers. Elijah Barber is shown preparing the land for a cornfield. The child is unidentified.

Two of the more prominent farm operators who cultivated many acres are now deceased. They were Zack C. Clarkson Sr. and John Rudisill. Clarkson lived on Bluff Road and Rudisill on Minervaville Road, the site of the old Minerva Academy. Both of these enterprising men were known around Hopkins for their successful farming operations. Unfortunately, pictures of their farming operations were unavailable.

Hopkins in its earlier years was mainly agricultural, and cotton was king. The area was made up of many small farms and some large ones. As time went by, many of the small farmers turned to other occupations, but some of the larger farms thrived. This photograph shows a farmer harvesting corn to be sold at the state farmers market.

The smokehouse was common on old farm sites. Farmers raised pigs, butchered them, and salted and smoked the meat. Butchering hogs was done on a cold day in winter. A farmer remembers his family "cooking and eating the liver and the tenderloin on butchering day because those pieces of meat were so good." Sausage, liver pudding, and hogshead cheese were made on that same day. Hams, sides of bacon, and shoulders were packed in salt until cured, then hung in the smokehouse. The smokehouse had no floor. A tub or container was placed on the ground in the center of the smokehouse and a small smoking fire made of hickory or oak wood was left to burn to smoke the meat and give it the desired flavor. (Courtesy of the South Carolina Department of Archives and History.)

Prior to the cotton gin, farmers could only grow long-staple cotton, also called sea-island cotton, around coastal areas. Short-staple cotton could be grown inland, but it had shorter fiber lengths that resulted in lesser quality, and the texture was less desirable due to seeds; removing them was a difficult and lengthy process. The introduction of the cotton gin made production much easier throughout the state. Coastal and inland farmers alike were able to gin cotton more quickly and efficiently, reducing the amount of manual labor needed. Pictured is what remains of an old cotton gin on Bluff Road.

Angus McGregor and his wife, Molly, started Laurinton Dairy in 1922. They originally sold milk and eggs to customers but eventually began selling milk to the Pet Milk Company. Angus and his son Rhett McGregor moved the farm to its present Hopkins location in 1938. Sam, the son of Rhett and Kate McGregor, graduated from Clemson with numerous agricultural honors and eventually took over the Laurinton Dairy. Sam is shown with some of his cows. (Courtesy of Sam and Betty McGregor.)

Milk was transferred to refrigerated stainless steel tanks. Dairy trucks came regularly to pump the milk into their own transferable tanks and take it for pasteurization. It became difficult for dairy farmers to connect with large dairy companies, as they eventually stopped taking new customers. One way to get an account with a large dairy company was to be grandfathered in from a retiring farmer's existing account. (Courtesy of Sam and Betty McGregor.)

Crops, including oats, rye, and pea vine hay, were planted to feed Holstein cattle. Coastal Bermuda hay was added in the 1950s. Wheat was planted and sold to the Adluh Flour Mill. Sam Evans McGregor was the last operator of the Laurinton Dairy. He was named one of four Outstanding Farmers in America in 1964. This photograph shows Sam's father, Rhett McGregor, (right) and a friend examining a grain crop. (Courtesy of Sam and Betty McGregor.)

Only 2,000 people were involved in agriculture in Richland and Lexington Counties in 1980. By 1987, Lexington County had 702 farms, and Richland had only 326. After the Laurinton Dairy discontinued the milk operation, McGregor raised fine heifers for sale to other farmers. Pictured in 1950 are, from left to right, Angus McGregor (on horse), Rhett McGregor, Bob Bailey (longtime Richland County farm agent), and Sam McGregor. (Courtesy of Sam and Betty McGregor.)

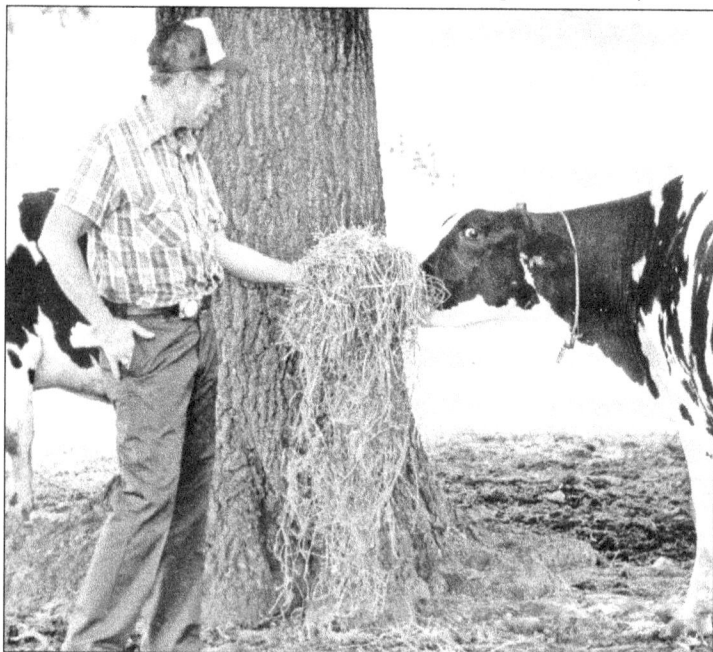

In 1986, South Carolina farmers suffered a devastating drought, and Indiana farmers brought hay to relieve them. Sam McGregor is shown feeding this special hay to one of his cows as newspaper photographers snap pictures of this generous gift from Indiana. His cows had just eaten sweet feed and were not hungry for the hay. This picture shows Sam trying to coax one of his cows to eat the hay for the camera. (Courtesy of Sam and Betty McGregor.)

This 1940 photograph shows an aerial view of the McGregor farm. This was the site of the McGregor dairy, which is seen in the picture, as are sheds, a barn, and other buildings necessary to the farm and to run a dairy. Cows had to be milked twice each day, regardless of holidays. This was inconvenient but necessary at Christmastime and other special holidays. The McGregors' two-story family home can be seen in the center. Their farm was located on South Carolina Highway 37, which is now called Lower Richland Boulevard. Highway 378, which goes to Sumter, runs parallel to the McGregor farm. The farm is approximately one-tenth of a mile from the highway. Lower Richland High School is on the other side of Highway 378, directly across from the McGregor farm. (Courtesy of Sam and Betty McGregor.)

This picture shows combining on the McGregor farm. This machine combines harvesting and threshing small grain crops. Prior to combines, farmers cut hay by hand or with a mowing machine and piled the hay in shocks (tepee-shaped stacks) or put it in a windrow to dry. When the hay was dry, a threshing machine separated the grain from the stalk. (Courtesy of Sam and Betty McGregor.)

An old Allis Chalmers hay baler is shown baling hay. This hay baler rolled small bales, which were easy to lift, but they were not easy to stack. Hay balers for square bales became more prevalent, as square bales are easier to stack and store. (Courtesy of Sam and Betty McGregor.)

Marion H. "Buddy" Hopkins is shown pulling his wagon on his grandparents' farm. This Clemson University honor graduate has been recognized as an excellent farmer by the South Carolina Soil Conservation Service for his soil and water practices with a sign placed on his farm. On March 27, 1989, this farm received a certificate and signs to be displayed in front of his home identifying it as a National Bicentennial Farm. To qualify for a National Bicentennial designation, the property must have been in continuous production by the same family for 200 years. In 1740, Marion's great-great-great-grandfather, John Hopkins, received the property in a land grant from the king of England. Originally indigo, cotton, rice, and corn were grown. At the present, Marion, with help from Marion Jr., produces corn, soybeans, wheat, oats, and barley. (Courtesy of Marion H. Hopkins.)

This is a photograph of a typical cotton house in Hopkins. Workers are unloading cotton from wagons to store in the house. Mules were used to pull these wagons and can been seen at right. A cotton house held cotton until the farmer had enough to gin. Cotton was picked every day and put in the house to store. Fifteen hundred pounds of seed cotton (cotton with seeds in it) was needed to turn out a 500-pound bale of lint cotton. It was taken to a gin and brought back

in bales similar to hay bales. When the cotton was baled, it was ready to sell. The cotton was later taken to platforms at the railroad, where it was sold and taken to town by train. Farmers would be left with 1,000 pounds of cottonseeds, which could be kept or sold to make cottonseed oil and feed. (Courtesy of Jack and Miriam Claytor.)

Corn was an important and common crop. This was a less time-consuming staple to grow, as it could be sown by hand and tended with a hoe rather than special or more expensive equipment. From small farms to large plantations, corn was a mainstay for every family's garden. Leroy Williams (left) and Joseph Carlton Derrick are pictured during a harvest day.

Large farms in the area planted a variety of crops, including corn, oats, rye, coastal bermuda, soybeans, and peavine hay. Production varied based on climate and methods of cultivation. Above, Sam McGregor (right) and an unidentified friend examine an early corn crop. Corn husks, stalks, and cobs were not thrown away. Instead, they were used to supplement livestock feed. (Courtesy of Sam and Betty McGregor.)

84

This building was once an office for Dr. Louis Tiffany Claytor, son of Dr. Hubert Claytor. Located outside of Woodside, the Claytor family home, it was later turned into a gift shop. Virginia Claytor Manning owned and operated the store during the early 1980s. Although no longer in operation, the building is still visible from the road.

The post office was originally located in the depot and then in a small wooden building behind Gorman's Store. It was later moved to the corner of Mustard's General Store and eventually to its present location on Lower Richland Boulevard. The Hopkins Post Office has 11 routes serving more than 5,000 families who have a Hopkins address, due to the widespread growth in the outlying areas.

Dr. Hubert Claytor came to Hopkins from Maryland early in his professional career. He was a well-regarded physician who made house calls by horse and buggy. His home, Woodside, was named to honor his childhood home of the same name. He had an office inside his home with a side entrance for patients. Dr. Hubert Claytor is pictured in his strawberry patch in Hopkins. (Courtesy of Jack and Miriam Claytor.)

Four

CONGAREE NATIONAL MONUMENT
HISTORY MADE IN NATURE

Congaree National Park consists of 26,000 acres of floodplain forest, 15,010 acres of which is a National Wilderness Area. It is part of the South Atlantic Coastal Plain Biosphere Reserve, a Globally Important Bird Area, and a Wetland of International Importance.

Wealthy planters from the Lowcountry introduced the plantation system to the region following the end of the Cherokee War and the establishment of Columbia as South Carolina's capital. Dikes were constructed to protect the fertile swamplands for farming. Small farmers could not compete with the coastal planters and moved inland to obtain farmland. Much of the land near the Congaree River was already sold, so some farmers used the swampland bordering the river to grow their cash crops, including cotton and tobacco. The considerable cost in the building and upkeep of dike systems led to the decline of large-scale farming in the area. Dead River Dike is 4 to 5 feet high and runs 2,000 feet by 800 feet, with several divisions caused by erosion. Cattle mounds were also constructed at this time, such as Cattle Mount No. 6 (below). (Both, courtesy of the South Carolina Department of Archives and History.)

Cattle mounds were built by early settlers in the Congaree Swamp to protect livestock from flooding. This gave the animals a safe place to graze, as they were an important source of both income and provisions. Cooner's Cattle Mount stands 5 to 10 feet high with a 300-foot circumference leading to the Brady property. The center shows an excavation pit from a 1978 archaeological study. (Courtesy of the South Carolina Department of Archives and History.)

Dead River Cattle Mount is oval in shape and stands only 3 to 5 feet high with a 250-foot circumference. The measurements and shapes of the mounds are central in determining early settlement patterns in the area. The top of the mound is rich in hardwood trees and vegetation. (Courtesy of the South Carolina Department of Archives and History.)

All of the cattle mounds in the Congaree Swamp were constructed from 1800 to 1900, with Brady's Cattle Mount being the most recent. Built by current owner Jack Brady's grandfather, it is still in use as a sanctuary for grazing animals. The flat top of the mound is covered with tall grass, but trees do not grow there due to its constant use. It stands 6 to 7 feet high and is oval in shape. (Courtesy of the South Carolina Department of Archives and History.)

Big Lake Cattle Mount is much smaller, being a 75-by-35-foot rectangle 2 feet high. The slope of the sides is approximately 45 degrees. This is common for most of these structures, allowing easy access for the animals while protecting them from the occasional swampland flooding. (Courtesy of the South Carolina Department of Archives and History.)

Mounds, dikes, and bridge abutments provide the only existing evidence of agricultural adaptation to a swamp environment in the state. The structure, design, workmanship, and materials of the mounds remain almost entirely unchanged, granting them a high degree of historical integrity. Their deterioration is due almost entirely to the fact that they are not protected from the elements, so they are vulnerable to weather, rooting animals, and erosion. Their integrity, from an historical standpoint, outweighs the effects of deterioration due to their relatively unspoiled settings. Cook's Lake Cattle Mount is shown here. (Courtesy of the South Carolina Department of Archives and History.)

James Adams received a land grant of more than 4,000 acres in the Congaree Swamp in 1839. He began erecting a dike system now known as the Northwest Boundary Dike to control the flooding and preserve land for future cultivation. Upon his death in 1841, his will divided the land equally between his four children. His instructions noted that they were to sell it to his brothers if they were not going to continue his project. The construction remains unfinished today. (Courtesy of the South Carolina Department of Archives and History.)

This 3-to-4-foot-high earthen dike runs northwest-to-southeast for approximately 650 feet and is interrupted by a gut of water before continuing for approximately 1,300 to 1,400 feet. The structure is covered with vegetation and hardwoods, many more than 150 years old. The Southwest Boundary Dike remains on the southwest side of the swamp and is thought to have been constructed during the 1840s as well. (Courtesy of the South Carolina Department of Archives and History.)

Meat was the mainstay of most diets and also a staple of cash income. Hogs were especially important prior to the Civil War. Hogs still tread throughout the swamp today, only now in a protected environment rather than as livestock to eat and sell at market each fall. Hogs, as rooting animals, have been one of the factors affecting the condition of the cattle mounds.

Cows also provided a means of food and income for the settlers and were well fed by the abundant forest vegetation. Owners earmarked their cattle for clear identification, and most made weekly trips to give them salt and to work on generating a calm temperament. Each fall, the farmers would transport large herds to the markets in Charleston.

Settlers made use of accessible Native American trading paths and extended roads and ferries across the swamp to haul livestock to markets. These four abutments are thought to be the remains of a bridge connected with a road and ferry system built by Isaac Huger in the 1780s. (Courtesy of the South Carolina Department of Archives and History.)

Congaree National Monument is home to at least eight species of woodpeckers. The pileated woodpecker, shown here, is often mistaken for the ivory-billed woodpecker. Visitors and birders alike wait patiently to photograph the birds in expectation of catching a glimpse of the rare ivory-billed woodpecker. This species has been near extinction since the 1930s.

This 1956 photograph shows cattle grazing. Cattlemen would pay rent to swamp owners to allow their cattle to graze in the fertile lands of the swamp, which helped reduce the expenses of feeding cattle and maintaining pastureland for large herds.

While grazing cattle in the swampland helped the farmer economically, his cattle were not forgotten. Weekly or biweekly trips were made to check the location, health, and safety of the herd and to make sure there was adequate grass for grazing. This picture, taken in the early 1950s, shows a herd of cows peacefully grazing in the swamp. A cattleman who kept cows in the Congaree Swamp kept a close eye on the weather and a close ear to the weather forecast. He needed to know if and when the Congaree River would rise, how high it would rise, and when the river would crest. The Congaree would crest in Columbia about 24 hours before it crested in Hopkins. If a big flood was predicted, the cattleman went into the swamp, found his cows, and drove them out of the swamp to higher ground and safety.

The Congarees used a slash-burn method of agriculture, slashing with crude stone implements to mark trees and burning them to clear a field for planting. Crops grew easily in the swamplands due to the fertile soil left by floodwaters. Sticks and bone tools were used for digging and planting. Their houses were built of wooden posts, daubed walls, and grass roofs.

European settlers arrived in the 1700s; unfortunately, they also brought with them a smallpox epidemic that wiped out the majority of the Congaree tribe. The remaining Congarees lived around Notchee Gut, later moving into Lexington County. They settled near the Fort Congaree trading post. The king of England provided land grants to many of the new inhabitants, including Virginia native John Hopkins.

The swamp has been used as a hiding place for runaway slaves, escaped convicts, moonshine whiskey stills, and even family valuables during Gen. William T. Sherman's march. There are several confirmed sightings of exotic wildlife, including panthers, cougars, and bears. Two rare birds, the Swainson's warbler and the Mississippi kite, breed in the swamp.

Gen. Francis Marion, widely known as the "Swamp Fox" of the Revolutionary War, eluded the British troops in the depths of the Congaree Swamp in 1776. An excerpt taken from one of his journals reads, "I look at the venerable trees around me and I know that I must not dishonor them."

In July 2001, Congaree National Monument was declared a Globally Important Bird Area. This is a well-deserved award, as more than 170 species of birds have been sighted. The great blue heron, coopers hawk, northern bobwhite, wood duck, bald eagle, barred owl, ruby-throated hummingbird, scarlet tanager, swamp sparrow, and dark-eyed junco are just a few of the species that have made the monument their home. Pictured above is a Carolina wren.

The 24,395-acre park encompasses 11,000 of the 13,000 acres of existing floodplain in South Carolina. The bottomland old-growth hardwood forest is said to be the largest in the country. The indisputable air of tranquility and natural beauty is found in a surprisingly short distance from the state's capital city. Its close proximity to Columbia makes it a desirable location for future floodplain science.

There have been at least 50 species of fish and 53 reptile and amphibian species confirmed, thanks in part to the profusion of wet areas. The spotted turtle, nonvenomous king and pinewood snakes, and venomous copperhead, canebrake rattlesnake, cottonmouth, and coral snake have been sighted. Gar and largemouth bass live in the streams and ponds. Irvin Portee is shown paddling in the Congaree. (Courtesy of the Barber family photograph collection.)

Some favorite pastimes of many people in the area are hunting and fishing. Favorite fish found in local waters, ponds, and creeks are bream, crappie, gar, catfish, and mudfish. Fishing is allowed within all areas of Congaree National Park for anyone bearing a current fishing license.

Moonshiners operated in the woods on high land, but many stills were run up and down the Congaree River in the lush protection of the Congaree Swamp. Tin tubs, copper tubing, and broken mason jars all tell the tale that moonshine was once produced here. The remains of an old moonshiner's still are visible from the boardwalk in Congaree National Park.

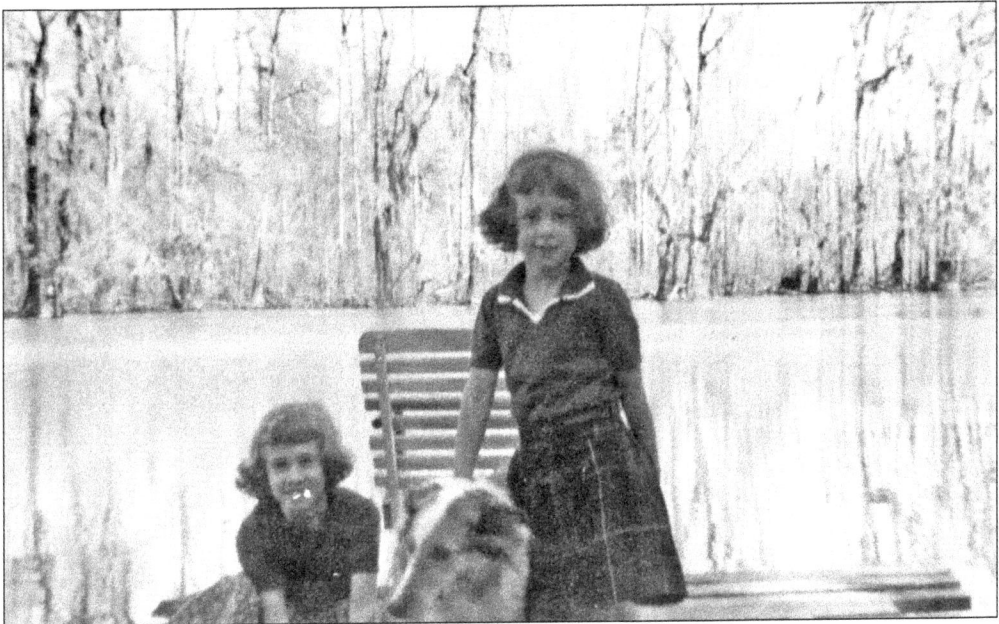

Many people in the Hopkins area have enjoyed the swamp for leisure time, fishing, picking blackberries, exploring, walking, looking for unusual plants that grow in the damp areas, and admiring the area's natural beauty. Old-timers were said to take the day off after they planted their cotton and spend it fishing at Goose Pond. This 1955 photograph shows children enjoying an afternoon at Goose Pond in Claytor Swamp.

The first inhabitants of the Congaree Swamp were prehistoric hunters and gatherers. The Congaree Indians were the next group to populate the region. Early Spanish explorer Hernando do Soto traveled throughout the area in 1540 during his quest for gold and recorded his fascination with the area and its wildlife in his journals.

Another explorer, John Lawson, along with his team of six Englishmen, three Native American males, and a squaw, made a 59-day voyage from Charleston through North and South Carolina, including the Congaree Swamp. He noted that the Congaree tribe had dwindled to a small number from disease but was intrigued by the storks and cranes they kept as pets.

Bald cypress became a target for logging. Francis Beidler, owner of the Santee River Cypress Lumber Company, acquired much of the land by 1905. Logging commenced, but difficult access to tracts near waterways limited the efforts. Operations halted within 10 years, which left the area virtually unscathed. (Courtesy of Congaree Action Now.)

There were thoughts of resuming logging in 1969 when timber prices escalated. The Sierra Club launched a grassroots campaign, supported by many local families. Congress designated the area the Congaree Swamp National Monument in 1976. This protected the area from loggers but not from Hurricane Hugo in 1989.

Champion trees in the park include a loblolly pine that is more than 100 years old, 14.66 feet in circumference, and 167 feet tall; a deciduous holly (3.1 feet in circumference and 38 feet tall), a laurel oak (22.08 feet in circumference and 130 feet tall), a swamp tupelo (15.7 feet in circumference and 132 feet tall), a sweet gum (16.9 feet in circumference and 160 feet tall), and a water hickory (16.5 feet in circumference and 143 feet tall). (Courtesy of *South Carolina Wildlife* magazine, November–December 1974.)

Harry Hampton wrote a column on preservation of the floodplains for the *State* newspaper in the 1950s. His opinions on conservation were not popular in his time, but his forethought made an incredible impact. His perseverance initiated a grassroots campaign eventually leading to the establishment of Congaree National Monument in 1976. Hampton is shown next to one of the champion trees in Congaree National Park. (Courtesy of Eddie Finley.)

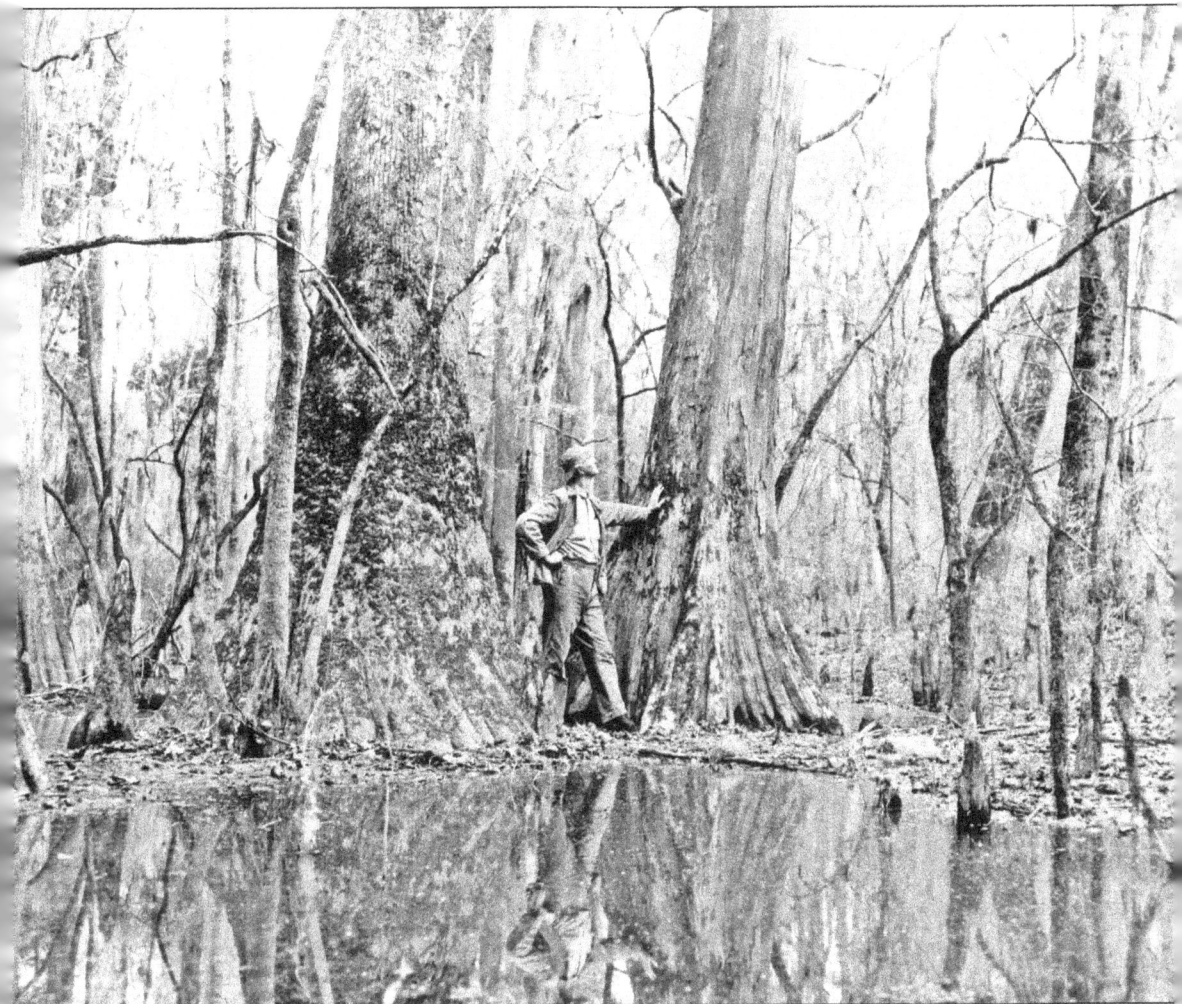

Harry R. E. Hampton was born in 1897 and was raised in Columbia and Charleston, South Carolina. His interest in the outdoors started at an early age, as he explored, hunted, and fished throughout the state. Hampton was a dedicated lifelong conservationist for the Congaree. The visitor's center at Congaree National Park now bears his name. (Courtesy of Eddie Finley.)

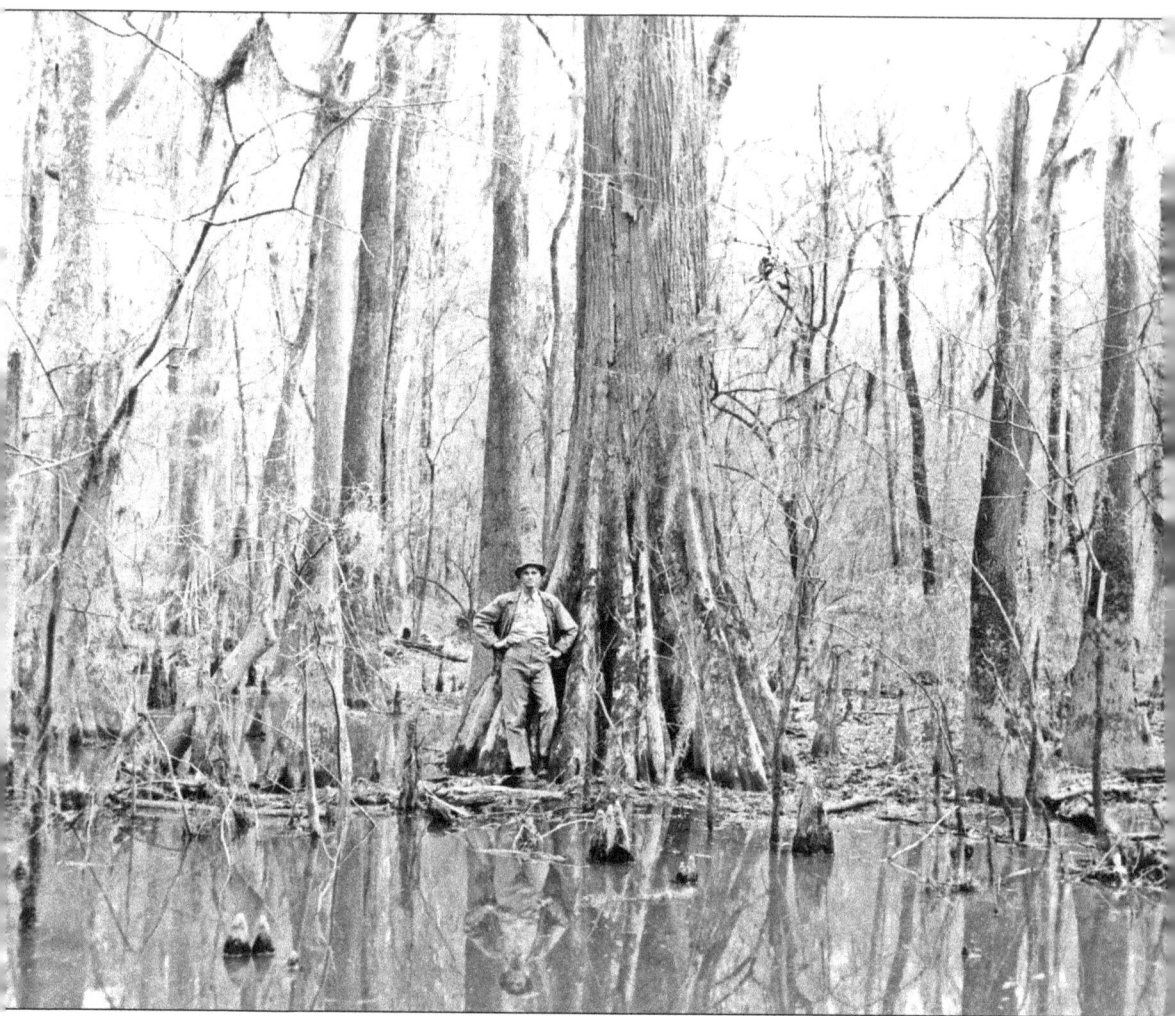

Harry Hampton is shown next to a bald cypress; this particular tree is now known as the Harry Hampton Tree in his honor. This tree is the largest bald cypress in the grove, boasting a height of 133 feet and a circumference of almost 24 feet. Hampton used this tree to illustrate to politicians, citizens, and the National Park Service what would be lost if this area were not preserved. (Courtesy of Eddie Finley.)

Harry Hampton initiated a campaign to organize a game and fish association, initiated natural resources legislation, and formed a state game commission later called the South Carolina Wildlife Federation. His persistence with legislation led to the formation of the State Wildlife Department and Commission in South Carolina in 1952. (Courtesy of Eddie Finley.)

This photograph shows the first visitor's center at Congaree National Park. This building now holds documents and archives pertaining to the history of the park. Classes are held here, and research facilities are available by appointment. The spacious new Harry Hampton Visitor's Center houses a wealth of information for park guests. Lifelike replicas of champion trees tower in the center of the main room, with artifacts and detailed historical information at every turn. Maps and self-guided tour information are available to aid in education about the forest even without an escort.

On September 21, 1989, Hurricane Hugo struck the South Carolina coast with 138-mile-per-hour winds and 20-foot storm surges. Hugo was the strongest storm to strike the East Coast north of Florida since Hazel in 1954. The damage was not contained to coastal areas; devastating losses were reported as far as 200 miles into the state. (Courtesy of the National Park Service.)

Hurricane Hugo leveled many trees; although this at first seemed to be irreparably damaging, fallen trees have since provided shelter for a variety of living organisms. The light was able to shine through the areas one canopied by treetops, promoting new growth on the forest floor. (Courtesy of the National Park Service.)

Congaree National Park, considered
the best remaining tract of old-growth
bottomland hardwood forest on the East
Coast, was in the path of Hurricane Hugo
in 1989. Many of the boardwalks that
greet visitors and provide paths for birding
and exploration in Congaree National
Park were splintered during the storm.
(Courtesy of the National Park Service.)

Hurricane Hugo tore through the
Midlands with wind speeds between 100
and 110 miles per hour. Many tall trees
were lost, and extensive damage was
done to the boardwalks by fallen trees
and high water. While the trees could
not be replaced, Congaree National Park
has rebuilt and maintains boardwalks
throughout the park, allowing visitors to
enjoy close observation of artifacts, plants,
and animals in natural surroundings that
would be difficult to access otherwise.
(Courtesy of the National Park Service.)

Congaree National Monument was named an International Biosphere Reserve by the United Nations Educational, Scientific, and Cultural Organization on June 30, 1983. Aside from housing bald cypress, water oak, sycamore, tupelo, and cottonwood trees, the park lays claim to one of the tallest temperate deciduous forests in the world. The average canopy in the monument is more than 100 feet. This is taller than the old-growth forests in the Himalayas, southern South America, and all of Eastern Europe. It is also home to the National Champion Loblolly Pine, standing an impressive 167 feet tall and 15 feet in circumference. (Courtesy of Congaree National Park.)

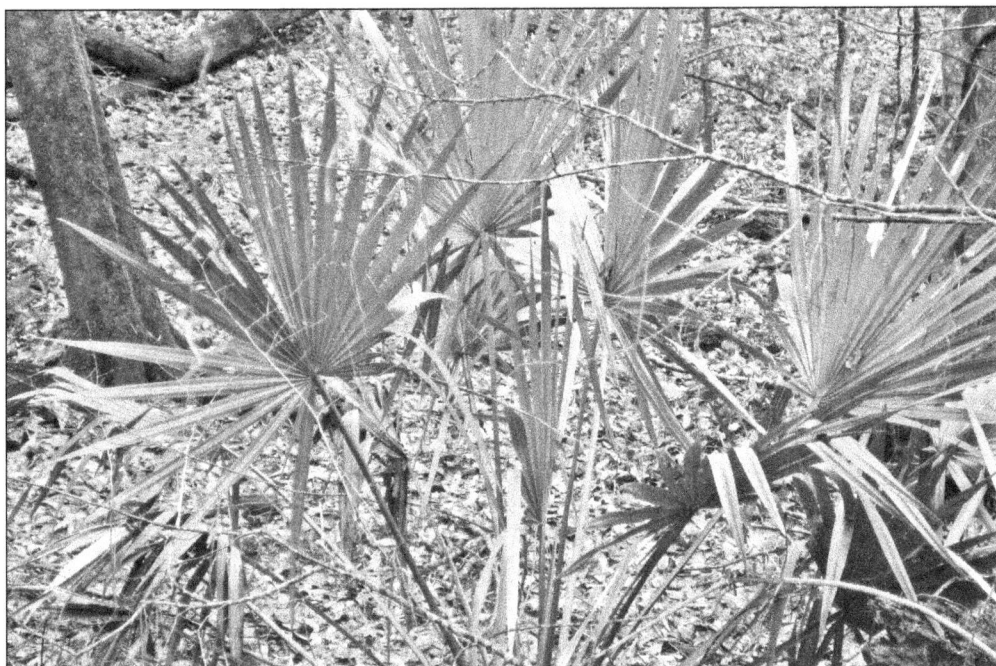

Saw palmettos grow in a variety of environments but thrive in flatland forests and marshes. The fruit of the saw palmetto is loved by black bears, white-tailed deer, and feral hogs. Native Americans once gathered the fruit as a staple of their diet. Today the fruits are collected for homeopathic remedies that may help prevent certain types of cancer.

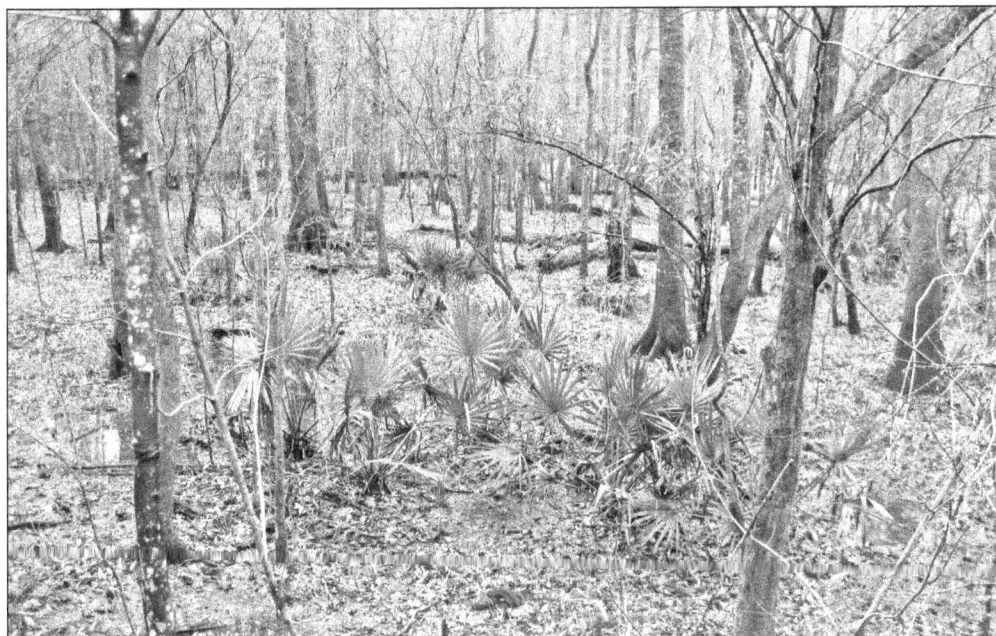

The saw palmetto, named for its sharp, saw-toothed leaf, is a dominant ground cover in southeastern forests and has been known to cover hundreds of acres. It tends to grow in clumps of 40 feet or more in diameter. It is predominantly found in the southeast and is sometimes confused with the dwarf palmetto. Clumps of saw palmettos are a favorite hiding place for rattlesnakes and wasps.

Bald cypress trees typically have precise demands for regeneration; however, in the Congaree Swamp forests, they are rapidly renewable. Their extensive root systems make them much less susceptible to being blown down than hardwood tree varieties. The biggest bald cypress in the park is almost 28 feet in circumference.

Cypress knees, which are part of the trees' root systems, clearly distinguish the bald cypress from the other trees in the forest landscape. Some knees in the Congaree have been found up to 7.5 feet high. Buttressed bases are also a distinctive identifying mark of this tree species.

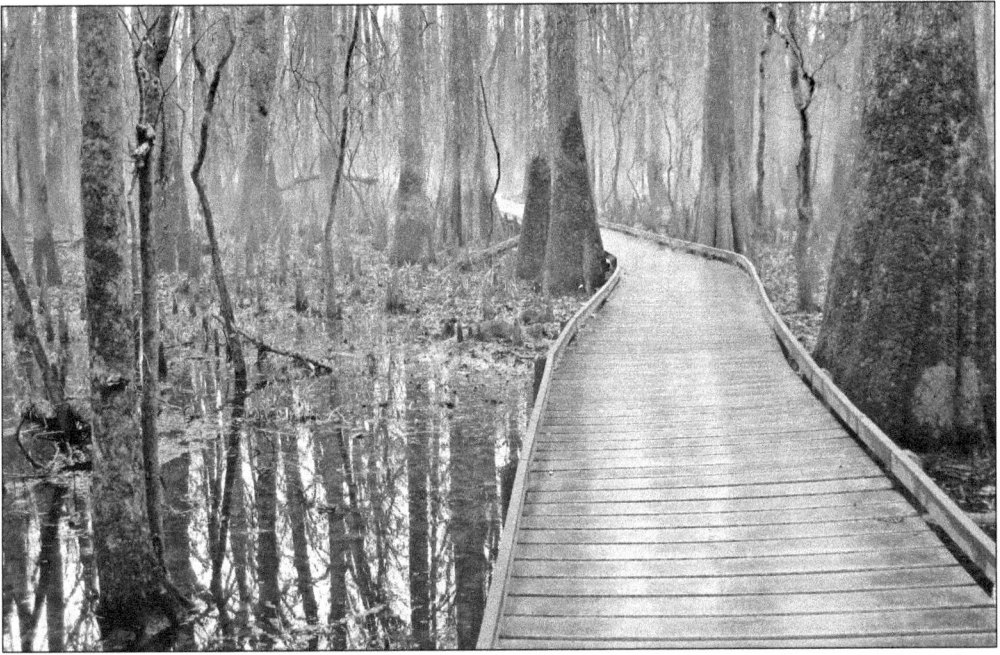

Flooding is most common in February and March, with episodes lasting only around three days. Occasionally, a major hurricane or tropical storm can send flooding rains, especially during the late summer and early fall. Although it is technically a swamp, it is more accurately called a river-bottom hardwood forest.

The boardwalk leading to Weston Lake is at a higher elevation than most of the other boardwalks and so is less susceptible to submerging. Some of the other raised boardwalks can become completely submerged. Water lines mark the levels of recent flooding.

Most of the park's forest is situated on the floodplain. Periodic flooding is not damaging to this ecosystem; rather, flooding plays a vital role in the natural balance of floodplain forests like the Congaree. Heavy flooding can cause slight damage, but flooding episodes typically induce only minor inconveniences.

Roughly 10 flooding events can be expected yearly. This allows the deposit of nutrients essential for growth and development of the bionetwork. Water tupelo and bald cypress are two tree species that flourish in standing or gently flowing water, as evidenced by their robust presence in Congaree National Park.

Part of what makes Congaree National Park so unique is that it contains the most extensive remaining tract of old-growth river-bottom hardwood forest in the southeast. Approximately 11,000 acres have never been used for any commercial gain.

The high canopy includes sweet gums, tupelo, hackberry, elm, and ash. Some oaks and hickory trees are also in the high canopy. These trees make it difficult for summer sun to shine through. The sub-canopy is comprised of red mulberry, red maple, American holly, and some minor species.

The forest floor has much smaller tree species and shrubs. Examples of these are pawpaw, ironwood, spicebush, strawberry bush, and switch cane. Some grasses grow where there are long, open areas beneath the understory.

It is unusual to see loblolly pines mixed with hardwoods in floodplains. The loblollies were able to survive with the hardwoods due to past disturbances in ecological patterns. The exact disturbances remain unclear.

Congaree National Park lies on the Congaree River. The vitality of the ecosystem is dependent upon the healthy state of the river, which explains the need to control pollution in the area.

Large, hollow trees in the Congaree Swamp are home to many small animals, such as squirrels, raccoons, and opossum. These natural homes provide necessary shelter from the elements as well as camouflaged safety from predators. It is not uncommon to spot one of these creatures inside their hollow hole while in Congaree National Park.

In a 2008 study, core samples were collected from several tree species, including loblolly pine, bald cypress, tupelo gum, ash, oak, and sycamore. All pine trees and most bald cypress were shown to be post-Colonial, dating between 100 and 300 years old. Growth patterns showed both positive and negative inflections, corresponding with climate patterns, Hurricane Hugo, logging, and ownership patterns even more than flooding effects.

The huge fallen trees in the swamp provide an unusual opportunity to view the root system of these mammoths. It is hard to conceive that these trees would give way to wind, water, and the powerful forces of nature. It is arresting to imagine how extensive the root system left beneath the ground must be.

The Congaree River is formed by the union of the Broad and Saluda Rivers. The Congaree joins the Wateree southeast of Columbia in the Santee. The Congaree Swamp is one of the last great untouched swamps in the South. Its 700-year-old cypress, great pine, and oak trees have been called the "forest of champions, the redwoods of the East."

In 1995, the Congaree Swamp superintendent had to turn away schools from visiting because the dirt roads were not suited to handle the traffic. The number of yearly visitors was extremely limited for this reason. It seemed that all possible resources had been considered, until a staff member suggested turning to the National Guard for assistance.

Sfc. Lewis Prettyman explained to the superintendent that the South Carolina National Guard is an avid supporter of local projects in conjunction with helping the troops meet their training requirements. So an alliance was formed, and the National Guard began work on what would be an extensive project.

124

Work began in August 1998. The South Carolina Army and Air National Guard cleared 1.3 miles of forest to build road elevation and a paved two-lane road gracefully curving around the swamp. They also constructed a 10,000-square-foot welcome center. This building was later named the Harry Hampton Visitor's Center.

The park offers guided tours for small groups through the forest. Off of the marked trails are some of the largest trees in the Congaree. Big tree hikes, as they are called, allow visitors to see trees that are not easily visible from the walking paths. The best months for the 5- to 6-mile hike are November through March, since thicker undergrowth in the summer makes hiking more difficult.

Visitors to the swamp are able to see where the rising floodwaters have marked the trees. Flooding in the lowland of the Congaree Swamp is a common occurrence. Rainwater from North Carolina can flood the Congaree when no water has fallen in the Midlands. The Congaree's highest recorded flood level occurred on August 27, 1908. The river crested at 35.8 feet in Columbia.

Benches are strategically placed along the boardwalk for visitors to rest or reflect on the sights and sounds around them. The height of the boardwalk allows people to view the area when the water is somewhat higher than usual. The knowledgeable park rangers offer guided tours to explain the intricacies of the ecosystem to visitors.

When walking in Congaree National Park, one is impressed by things of the past—trees that have lived for hundreds of years, people who have hunted and fished these waters, runaway slaves that hid there to reach freedom, and the insightful leaders that fought to preserve this place of natural wonders. At the same time, thoughts of the future generations and the hope that they will inherit this place in its uniquely unaltered state of beauty are also present. As Congaree National Park and the town of Hopkins continue to grow, may the traditions of the past preserve their most unique charm.

Visit us at
arcadiapublishing.com

www.ingramcontent.com/pod-product-compliance
Lightning Source LLC
Chambersburg PA
CBHW050635110426
42813CB00007B/1818